# Celebrate!

# France

Robyn Hardyman

# W
## FRANKLIN WATTS
LONDON•SYDNEY

This edition first published in 2009
by Franklin Watts

Copyright © 2009
The Brown Reference Group Ltd

Franklin Watts
338 Euston Road
London NW1 3BH

Franklin Watts Australia
Level 17/207 Kent Street
Sydney, NSW 2000

A CIP catalogue record for this book is available from the British Library.
Dewey no: 914.4

ISBN 978 0 7496 8427 3          914.4

Printed in China

Franklin Watts is a division of Hachette Children's Books, an Hachette UK company.
www.hachette.co.uk

Note to parents and teachers concerning websites:
In the book every effort has been made by the Publishers to ensure that websites are suitable for children, that they are of the highest educational value, and that they contain no inappropriate or offensive material. However, because of the nature of the Internet, it is impossible to guarantee that the contents of these sites will not be altered. We advise that Internet access is supervised by a responsible adult.

**For The Brown Reference Group Ltd**
Project Editor: Sarah Eason
Designer: Paul Myerscough
Picture Researcher: Maria Joannou
Indexer: Claire Throp
Design Manager: David Poole
Managing Editor: Miranda Smith
Editorial Director: Lindsey Lowe

**Consultant Editor**
Peter Lewis
Writer and Editor for the American Geographical Society, New York

**Author**
Robyn Hardyman

# Contents

# Welcome to France

France is the biggest country in western Europe. It is extremely beautiful and has a wide variety of landscapes, from winding rivers and high mountains to rolling fields and sandy beaches. France has a long and fascinating history, and a great tradition of culture. Today it is a wealthy country with a strong economy.

France

United Kingdom

Belgium

Germany

France

Luxembourg

Switzerland

Italy

Spain

Andorra

Monaco

The Eiffel Tower in Paris is one of the most famous landmarks in the world – it is so famous that it has become a symbol of France. It was designed by Gustave Eiffel and built in 1889 to mark the **centenary** of the French Revolution. Eiffel also designed the Statue of Liberty in New York.

## Marianne – symbol of France

A female figure called Marianne is a national symbol of France. She stands for reason, liberty and the ideals of the French Republic. Marianne first appeared during the French Revolution in paintings, leading the revolutionaries to freedom. Today, she appears on the official state logo (right), as well as banknotes, stamps and coins.

Liberté • Égalité • Fraternité
**RÉPUBLIQUE FRANÇAISE**

## French borders

France borders the sea in the north and west. It has land borders to the east and south with Belgium, Luxembourg, Germany, Switzerland, Italy, Monaco, Andorra and Spain.

## FRENCH FACTS

| | |
|---|---|
| FULL NAME | French Republic |
| CAPITAL CITY | Paris |
| AREA | 547,029 square km |
| POPULATION IN 2008 | 64,058,000 |
| MAIN LANGUAGE | French |
| MAIN RELIGION | Roman Catholic |
| CURRENCY | Euro |

## Eiffel Tower

Every year, millions of tourists visit the famous Eiffel Tower in Paris.

## National emblem

This is the national **emblem** of France. It has been widely used since 1953 and it appears on the front cover of the French passport.

# History Highlights

*France has a long and interesting history. It has been fought over by many countries. In 1789, there was a violent revolution, which overthrew the monarchy. France is now controlled by an elected president.*

France is one of the oldest **democracies** in the world. It became a democracy after a **revolution** in 1789. Later that year, a document called the 'Declaration of the Rights of Man and the Citizen' was published. It stated that all French people would live under the rules of liberty and **equality**.

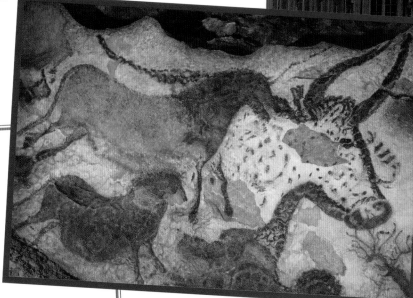

## Lascaux

In 1940, four boys found a series of caves at Lascaux in southern France. On the cave walls were hundreds of amazing paintings, made 17,000 years ago by France's earliest inhabitants. They show hunting scenes, cattle, horses and deer.

**WEB LINKS** ▼▼▼▼▼▼▼▼▼▼▼▼
For more information and a virtual tour of the caves at Lascaux go to:
www.culture.gouv.fr/culture/arcnat/lascaux/en/

## Louis XIV

Five **dynasties** ruled France after the Franks. King Louis XIV (reigned 1643–1715) came from the Bourbon dynasty. During his reign France became the most powerful country in Europe. Louis built a great palace at Versailles, near Paris. It was a centre of culture and a symbol of power. Louis is considered France's greatest **monarch**.

## *Early history*

The ancient Romans named France Gaul after the Gauls, the ancient Celtic people who lived there. The Romans conquered Gaul and made it part of their empire in the first century B.C.E. The modern French language developed from Latin, the language of the Romans. The Romans ruled France for 500 years, but were eventually defeated by a powerful tribe called the Franks. The name France comes from the Franks.

**DID YOU KNOW?**
Many plays, ballets and concerts were performed at the court of Louis XIV at Versailles. Here, the king himself is taking part in a ballet. He is dressed up as the Sun.

## Revolution

In 1789, the French people became very angry because their king, Louis XVI, kept forcing them to pay more money in **taxes**. They swept away the government in a violent revolution and set up their own **parliament** called the National Assembly. In a terrible time known as the 'Reign of Terror', up to 40,000 people were killed, including Louis XVI and his queen, Marie Antoinette. A general in the army, Napoleon Bonaparte, finally took control. In 1804 he declared himself the **emperor** of France.

### Bastille

The Bastille prison in Paris was attacked by the revolutionaries on 14th July 1789 and the prisoners were freed. France still celebrates its National Day on 14th July every year.

### *Marie Antoinette*

As French peasants struggled to feed their families, they had become increasingly angry at stories of expensive clothes and parties held by Queen Marie Antoinette at Versailles. In 1793, the revolutionaries took action, and the queen was beheaded on the guillotine.

## Napoleon Bonaparte

Napoleon Bonaparte (1769–1821) was a great military leader who became a strong ruler of France. He invaded other countries in Europe to create an empire. He ruled this empire from 1804 to 1814, and again for several months in 1815. He was finally defeated in 1815 by Britain, Prussia, Russia and Austria at the Battle of Waterloo.

## War and recovery

In the nineteenth century, the **economy** of France grew as new industries developed. Railways were built to connect the different parts of the country. However, the early twentieth century was a terrible time for France. In World War I (1914–18) and World War II (1939–45) France was invaded by Germany and millions of soldiers died or were wounded. In the years since 1945, France has worked hard to become a rich and powerful country again. It has worked with other countries to create a strong **European Union** (EU).

The EU flag

9

# Fly the Flag

*The national flag of France has three vertical stripes of blue, white and red. It is usually known as the tricolore, which means 'three colours'. The blue side is attached to a flagpole.*

The tricolore flag was first used at the beginning of the French Revolution in 1789. Traditionally, blue and red were the colours of Paris, and white was the colour of the king. The new tricolore was the symbol of the French Revolution, and it then became the symbol of the First Republic in France. Originally, the stripes were not of equal widths. The red was the widest, then the white, then the blue. Napoleon Bonaparte changed the stripes to equal widths.

## DID YOU KNOW?

The three colours of the French flag represent different parts of French life and history. Blue is the colour of Saint Martin, a rich army officer who ripped his blue coat in half with his sword and gave half to a beggar in the snow. The blue also symbolizes the duty of the rich to care for the poor. White is the colour of the Virgin Mary, of French heroine Joan of Arc (shown left) and of royalty. Red is also the colour of Saint Denis, the patron saint of Paris.

**Try this!**

## Make a French flag

- On a piece of white card draw a rectangle that is exactly 22.5 cm long and 15 cm high.
- Carefully cut out the rectangle.
- Use a ruler to find the points that are 7.5 cm and 15 cm along the long sides of the rectangle.
- Draw vertical lines across the rectangle joining these points, so that your rectangle has three stripes of equal width.
- Use paint or felt-tip pens to colour in the left-hand stripe blue and the right-hand stripe red. Leave the centre stripe white.
- Use sticky tape to attach your flag to a pencil or a thin stick.

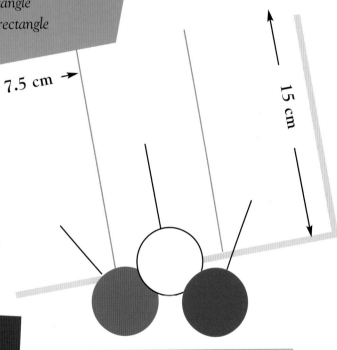

7.5 cm

15 cm

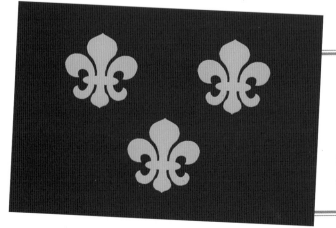

## Fleur-de-Lis

This was the flag of the kings of France in **medieval** times. The gold flowers are called fleurs-de-lis, which means 'flowers of the lily'.

# Hymn to France

*France's national anthem is La Marseillaise, 'Song of Marseille'. It is known around the world for its stirring words and rousing melody. La Marseillaise was written during the French Revolution. It was adopted as the national anthem in 1795.*

*L*a Marseillaise was written in April 1792, when France was at war with Austria and Prussia. The composer was a French army engineer, Claude-Joseph Rouget de Lisle. He called it *Marching Song of the Rhine Army*, after his **regiment**. In August 1792, revolutionary soldiers from the town of Marseille adopted it as their battle song. The song has been called *La Marseillaise* ever since.

### Song for France
Claude-Joseph Rouget de Lisle is portrayed singing *La Marseillaise*. De Lisle composed it overnight when he was asked to write a marching song for his unit.

## WEB LINKS

To hear *La Marseillaise* go to:

http://www.diplomatie.gouv.fr/en/IMG/wav/mars.wav

## Spirit of revolt

Since the days of the French Revolution, *La Marseillaise* has been sung in many other countries, including Russia. But in France it has been banned several times because of its revolutionary spirit. During World War II, when Nazi Germany occupied France, people were imprisoned or executed for singing *La Marseillaise*.

## Bastille Day

The **national anthem**, *La Marseillaise*, is sung on 14th July, Bastille Day, as fireworks light up the sky.

Words and music by
CLAUDE-JOSEPH ROUGET DE L'ISLE (1760 - 1836)

Al - lons en - fants de la Pa - tri - e, Le jour de

Con - tre nous de la ty - ran-

## La Marseillaise translation

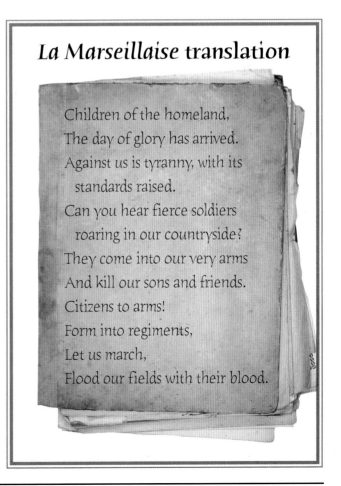

Children of the homeland,
The day of glory has arrived.
Against us is tyranny, with its
standards raised.
Can you hear fierce soldiers
roaring in our countryside?
They come into our very arms
And kill our sons and friends.
Citizens to arms!
Form into regiments,
Let us march,
Flood our fields with their blood.

# Regions of France

The landscape of France is varied and often spectacular. Its mountains are some of the highest in Europe. The northern coast has chalk cliffs and sandy beaches. In the south, the sunny Mediterranean coast attracts thousands of visitors. Inland, fertile farmland covers most of the country.

In the southwest, the dramatic Pyrenees Mountains form France's border with Spain. The magnificent Alps are in the southeast. They are among the highest mountains in the world. North of the Alps are the Jura Mountains. Their lower slopes are covered with forests.

## Wine country
In the valleys of rivers such as the Rhône, the fertile soil and climate are perfect for growing grapes to make wine.

### DID YOU KNOW?
France is a big country to travel across. The TGV ('*train à grande vitesse*' or 'high speed train') is France's high-speed rail service. TGV trains travel at speeds of 320 km/h, making long-distance travel across the country easier.

## Towering mountain

Mont Blanc, in the French Alps, is the highest mountain in Europe. Its **summit** is 4,807 metres high and marks the border between France and Italy.

## Climate

The climate of France is moderate. It is generally warmer and sunnier in the south than in the north. In the mountains it can get extremely cold. In the Rhône valley in the south, a strong, cold wind called the Mistral sometimes blows for several days during winter and spring. It can reach 96 km/h.

## FRENCH FACTS

| | |
|---|---|
| LONGEST RIVERS | Loire 1,020 km, Rhône 813 km |
| HIGHEST MOUNTAIN | Mont Blanc in the Alps 4,807 metres |
| LARGEST CITIES | Paris, Marseille, Lyon, Toulouse |

## Corsica

The beautiful island of Corsica in the **Mediterranean** Sea is part of France. Inland, Corsica has mountains and **gorges**. There are steep cliffs as well as beaches along the coast.

# What's Cooking?

*French food is famous around the world for its quality. The varying landscapes and climates of the regions of France mean that many different kinds of food are produced in different areas.*

France is particularly known for its delicious breads, cheeses, chocolates and cakes. The French claim they make at least 365 different kinds of cheese – one for every day of the year! They are proud of the regional **cuisine** traditions. Normandy in the north is famous for its rich cream, apples and seafood. Provence, in the south, uses tomatoes, olive oil, garlic and plenty of fresh herbs.

## Markets
Colourful outdoor markets in France sell fresh, locally produced food. Shoppers choose their fruit, bread, cheese and vegetables with great care.

**DID YOU KNOW?**
If you visit a French restaurant, you are likely to find some unusual items on the menu. In France, people eat snails (*les escargots*), frogs' legs (*les cuisses de grenouille*) and horsemeat (*le cheval*)!

## Cheese varieties

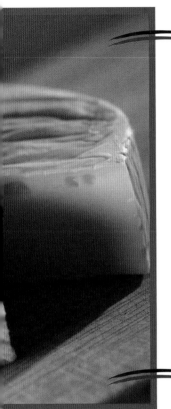

French cheeses come in a wide range of different textures and tastes. Camembert is a soft, runny cheese. Brie is another soft cheese, with a spongy texture, while Roquefort is a hard, crumbly cheese that has a blue and white colour.

## What's on the menu?

This special family lunch would probably last for several hours!

**vichyssoise**
cold leek and potato soup

**bœuf bourguignon and gratin dauphinoise**
rich beef stew and sliced potatoes baked with butter and cream

**salade verte**
salad leaves with olive oil and lemon juice

**brie and chèvre**
a soft, creamy cheese and a goat's cheese

**tarte tatin**
sweet pastry tart made with caramelized apples

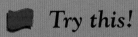 *Try this!*

## Let's make crêpes (pancakes)

*Ingredients:*
*125 g plain flour*
*pinch of salt*
*2 eggs*
*200 ml milk mixed with 85 ml water*
*60 g butter*
*caster sugar*
*lemon juice*

*Whisk together the flour, salt and eggs, then add the milk and water to make a smooth batter. Melt the butter in a pan. Add two tablespoons of it to the batter and pour the rest into a jug. Ask an adult to make a frying pan really hot. Pour a little melted butter into the hot pan, and then add two tablespoons of batter. Swirl it from side to side to cover the base. Cook for about 30 seconds. Flip the pancake over and cook the other side. Slide the pancake on to a plate. Sprinkle with caster sugar and lemon juice.*

# How Do I Say...?

*France is a large country, so the ways in which people pronounce the language, and even some of the words they use, varies from one region to another. People on the island of Corsica speak a language that is more like Italian than French.*

The Académie Française is an official organization designed to protect the French language from the influence of English. It is careful about adopting English words, such as 'le weekend'. The Académie wants to keep the French language pure.

**DID YOU KNOW?**
Some French words are commonly used in English. This is a street sign for rue du Rendez-Vous. *Rendez-vous*, a French word meaning 'appointment', is also used in the English language.

## Words and phrases

| English | French | How to say it |
|---------|--------|---------------|
| hello | bonjour | bon-joor |
| goodbye | au revoir | oh-rev-waar |
| please | s'il vous plaît | see-voo-play |
| thank you | merci | mare-see |
| yes | oui | wee |
| no | non | nong |
| How are you? | Comment allez-vous? | kommon-tallay-voo |
| My name is ... | Je m'appelle ... | zhe-mapell ... |

## Some slang expressions

**Un BCBG** (stands for *bon chic bon genre*) means a Parisian person who dresses smartly and expensively.

**J'ai la pêche** (I have the peach) means 'I'm full of energy'.

**J'ai le cafard** (I have the cockroach) means 'I'm down in the dumps'.

## French sayings

*Qui vole un oeuf, vole un bœuf.* 'He who steals an egg, steals an ox.' This is the equivalent of the English saying: 'Give him an inch and he'll take a mile'.

*Il ne faut pas vendre la peau de l'ours avant de l'avoir tué.* 'You mustn't sell the bear's skin before you have killed it.' This is the equivalent of the English saying: 'Don't count your chickens before they hatch'.

## French speaking countries

These children live in the African country of Senegal, but speak French. France ruled over Senegal until 1960. French is still its official language.

**WEB LINKS**
To see and hear more slang expressions go to:
http://french.about.com/library/express/blexpres.htm

# Stories and Legends

*French novels, plays and poems telling traditional stories from the past have become classics all over the world.*

France's oldest known piece of writing is *The Song of Roland*. No one knows exactly when it was written, but it is thought to have been during either the eleventh or twelfth century by an unknown poet. It tells the tale of the death of Roland, the nephew of Emperor Charlemagne. Roland is attacked on his return from Spain in 778 C.E., and he dies a hero's death.

## Beauty and the Beast

This French fairytale tells how Belle is forced to live in the Beast's castle. She falls in love with him, however, and when she sheds tears over him he is changed into a prince. Long ago, a fairy had turned him into a beast, but Belle's love for him breaks the evil spell.

RÉPUBLIQUE FRANÇA 18

HERNANI DE VICTOR HU

## Notre Dame

Victor Hugo's book *The Hunchback of Notre Dame* is set in the cathedral of Notre Dame in Paris. Notre Dame took 182 years to build. Building began in 1163 and only finished in 1345. With its many **gargoyles** and sculptures, it is one of the best examples of **Gothic** architecture.

## Victor Hugo

Victor Hugo (1802–85) was a French poet, playwright and novelist. In his popular novel *Les Misérables*, Hugo attacked **injustices** in society.

### *Musical story*

**In recent years *Les Misérables* has been produced as a very successful stage musical.**

# Art and Culture

*For hundreds of years, French artists and musicians have created great work in a country that prides itself on its cultural history.*

Claude Debussy (1862–1918) was a French composer. His music has been called Impressionist, because in it he tried to create an impression of things he saw in nature, such as moonlight or the sea. Debussy wrote music for the piano, for an orchestra, an **opera** and a ballet, *L'Après-midi d'un Faune* ('The Afternoon of a Faun').

### Sculpture
One of the most famous sculptors in the world is Auguste Rodin (1840-1917). His original bronze and marble statue 'The Thinker' can be seen in the Musée Rodin in Paris.

## Fashion
The French are known for their style and elegance. Fashion designers such as Coco Chanel, Christian Dior, Yves Saint Laurent, Jean-Paul Gaultier and Louis Vuitton are admired worldwide. Paris is one of the fashion capitals of the world.

## Claude Monet and the Impressionists

Claude Monet (1840–1926) was one of a group of French painters called the Impressionists. These painters tried to represent landscapes and other scenes spontaneously and naturally, and to capture the effects of natural light. 'Water Lilies', painted at his garden in Giverny, is one of Monet's most famous paintings.

## Cannes film festival

Every year the southern beach resort of Cannes hosts the best-known film festival in the world. Film-makers everywhere want to win its main prize, the Palme d'Or ('Golden Palm').

## WEB LINKS ▼▼▼▼▼▼▼▼▼▼▼▼▼▼▼▼▼▼

For more information on Monet and Giverny go to:
http://www.fondation-monet.com/uk/

# Make Your Own Stained-Glass Window

*You can make a stained-glass picture, just like the windows made by skilled craftsmen hundreds of years ago for the Gothic cathedrals of France, such as the one at Chartres.*

**You will need:**
- a piece of black card
- a pencil
- a craft knife
- paper
- scissors
- craft glue
- several sheets of different coloured tissue paper

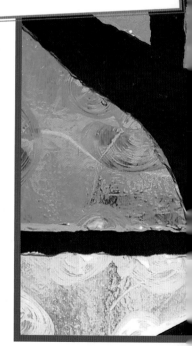

1 Plan your window design on the black card. It can be a simple pattern, or a picture of an object, or even the letters of your name. It should be bold and simple, as it will be made up of shapes cut out of card.

2 Using a pencil, draw the shapes of your design on to the black card. Keep a wide border of black card all around the edges. You also need to keep thick strips of black card between your coloured shapes. These must be attached to an edge, so that they stay in place.

3 Ask an adult to help you cut out the 'holes' in your design, using scissors or a craft knife.

4 Choose different coloured tissue paper to put over the holes in your design. Use a mixture of strong colours and paler ones, to give variety to your design.

5 Carefully cut the tissue paper into the shapes of the holes in the design, using scissors. Each piece must be slightly bigger than the hole, so that it can be stuck to the black card strips around the hole.

**6** Turn your window over so that the back is facing you. Put a little craft glue on the black card strips of the design. Carefully stick the pieces of tissue paper over the correct holes.

**7** Turn your window over again, to check the holes are properly covered. Allow the card to dry.

**8** When the glue is dry, put your card on or in front of a window so that the light shines through the tissue paper.

## Coloured windows

Stained-glass windows have been used in churches since at least 348 C.E. The oldest stained-glass windows that remain today are found in French churches dating from the twelfth century.

**DID YOU KNOW?**
Early stained-glass windows showed scenes from the Bible. They taught people about Christianity at a time when only monks were educated. Most ordinary people were unable to read or write.

# Sports and Leisure

*French workers have about five weeks' paid holiday each year. There are also thirteen days of national holidays a year. Leisure time is often spent with family and friends, in sports, cultural events and travel.*

French people love to sit outside a café and watch the world go by. The oldest coffee house in the world, Le Procope, opened in Paris in 1686. French writers, artists and students have always met in cafés to talk and to work. In rural villages, the café is at the heart of local life.

## Football

Football is the most popular sport in France. Both children and adults play, and fans support their local teams in competitions. In 1998, the French national team won the World Cup. The team reached the final again in 2006.

## DID YOU KNOW?

France is the most popular country in the world for tourists. It is visited by about 75 million visitors each year.

## Café life

The café is a sociable place, where French people enjoy spending time chatting and eating and drinking with neighbours and friends.

## Amélie Mauresmo

French tennis player Amélie Mauresmo (born 1979) is a world-class competitor. In 2006 she won the Wimbledon Championships and the Australian Open, and reached the semi-finals of the US Open.

## Tour de France

France's most famous sporting event is a cycle race called the Tour de France. It is held over a period of three weeks and covers a gruelling 3,500 km. The route travels around France, and into neighbouring countries. The finish line is always in the centre of Paris. Every summer, more than 150 cyclists from around the world compete in this event.

## Skiing

The French Alps are a popular skiing destination, for both the French people and for tourists.

## WEB LINKS ▼▼▼▼▼▼▼▼▼▼▼▼▼▼▼

For detailed information on the Tour de France go to:
http://www.letour.fr/us/homepage_horscourseTDF.html

# Festivals and Holidays

*French people celebrate many national and religious holidays. As well as the big events, there are hundreds of smaller, local festivals in the regions every year. These can be food festivals, or arts and music festivals.*

Bastille Day, on 14th July, is France's most important national holiday. It commemorates the storming of the Bastille prison in Paris on 14th July 1789. Every town and village in France celebrates, usually with street parties, dancing and fireworks.

## Wine festivals

France is famous for producing wine. It has about 10,000 square km of vineyards, and produces more wine than any other country apart from Italy. The grapes are harvested in the autumn. At this time many wine-producing regions celebrate with wine festivals.

## Bastille Day, Paris

On 14th July every year, a great military parade celebrating Bastille Day takes place on the Champs-Elysées in Paris.

## Religious festivals

More than 80 per cent of French people are Roman Catholic. National holidays are therefore often held during important religious festivals, including Easter, Christmas and All Saints' Day (1st November).

## Fruit festival

The southern French town of Menton celebrates its sunny climate every year with a festival of fruit, the Fête du Citron. Objects made from locally grown oranges and lemons decorate the town.

**DID YOU KNOW?**
*Fête* is the French word for 'festival'. The French celebrate their local saint's day with a *fête patronale*, and a village festival is called a *fête champêtre*.

# Glossary

**Bible** the religious text of the Christian and Jewish faiths

**centenary** 100th anniversary

**Christianity** the religion based on the teachings of Jesus Christ

**climate** the average weather conditions over a long period of time

**cuisine** a style of cooking

**democracies** countries run by governments voted for by the people

**dynasties** series of rulers from the same family

**economy** the way a country uses its money, goods and services

**equality** the principle by which all people should be treated in the same way

**emblem** symbol that represents a country

**emperor** the male ruler of an empire

**European Union** framework for economic and political cooperation between twenty-seven European countries

**fertile** describes rich soil that can produce lots of fruit and vegetables

**gargoyles** grotesque carved figures, which are used to project water away from the sides of buildings

**gorge** a deep, narrow canyon with steep, rocky walls

**Gothic** medieval style of architecture where the buildings feature pointed arches and high vaults

**guillotine** a machine used to cut off people's heads

**injustices** unfairnesses, wrongs

**liberty** personal freedom

**medieval** describes the Middle Ages; this period of history was from about 400 to 1450 C.E.

**Mediterranean** part of an area of Europe that is found around the Mediterranean Sea, includes countries such as Italy, France, Greece and Spain

**monarchs** kings or queens

**national anthem** official song of a country

**opera** play in which the words are sung to music instead of spoken

**parliament** assembly that makes a country's laws

**president** person who runs a country, voted for by its people

**regiment** a unit of soldiers within an army

**revolution** overthrow of a government by the people

**summit** highest point of a mountain

**taxes** money people must pay to support the actions of a government

# Find Out More

## Books

Crosbie, Duncan. *Find out about France.*
Franklin Watts
ISBN: 978 0 7496 7730 5

Deary, T. *Horrible histories – France.*
Scholastic
ISBN: 978 0 4399 7925 2

Fodor Travel Publications. *Fodor's Around
Paris with Kids.* Fodor's Travel
Publications Inc., U.S.
ISBN: 978 1400 01919 9

Ganeri , Anita and Wright, Rachel.
*www.franklinwatts.co.uk/
GEOGRAPHY_Books_COUNTRY-
TOPICS_Series_26389_55961.htm" \o
"Country Topics" Country Topics- France.*
ISBN: 978 0 7496 7328 4

Hodge, Susie. *Artists in their world Claude
Monet.* Franklin Watts
ISBN: 978 0 7496 6625 5

Ruth Thomson, *Living in – France.*
Franklin Watts
ISBN: 978 0 7496 6338 4

Tidmarsh, C. *Country Files – France*
Franklin Watts
ISBN: 978 0 7496 6416 9

## Websites

**http://uk.franceguide.com/maps/
france/regions**
This is the official site of the French
Government Tourist Office. The guide
to the regions is particularly useful.

**www.ambafrance –uk.org/kids**
The junior edition of The Embassy of
France website features colourful
articles and interactive games.

**www.letour.fr**
The official site of France's favourite
sporting event, the Tour de France,
features live commentary in July.

**www.musee-orsay.fr**
The collection of the Musée d'Orsay in
Paris includes works by modern artists.

**www.tour-eiffel.fr**
The official site of the Eiffel Tower has
virtual tours, information and games.

# Index